NATIONAL GEOGRAPHIC

T0080648

Communities
Across
America Today

SARAH GLASSCOCK

PICTURE CREDITS
Cover © 1993 Carmen Lomas Garza/Photo Credit M. Lee Fatherree;
page 1 1996 Lawrence Migdale/Photo Researchers, Inc; pages 2-3
D. R. Stoecklein/The Stock Market; pages 4-5 © 1996 David A. Barnes/
FPG; page 5 (top inset), 9 (top inset) Ben Marra; page 5 (center inset),
13 (top inset), page 11 (inset) © Michael Newman/ PhotoEdit; page 5
(bottom inset), 6 © David Young-Wolff/PhotoEdit; pages 6-7 © 1994
Jerry Driendl/FPG; pages 7, 21 © 1987 Carmen Lomas Garza/Photo
Credit Wolfgang Dietze; page 8 Rosemary Calvert/Stone; page 9 Robert
Cameron/Stone; pages 9 (center inset), 18 (inset) © Myrleen Ferguson/
PhotoEdit; (bottom inset) Vince Streano/Stone; page 10 © Jeff Foot/
Bruce Coleman, Inc, NY; page 11 © Richard Lord/PhotoEdit; page 12
James Randklev/Stone; page 13 © age fotostock; page 13 (bottom
inset) © Jeff Greenberg/PhotoEdit; page 14 Mike Yoder Lawrence/
Journal-World; page 15 Cotton Coulson; page 16 (top) © Patti
McConville/Midwestock; page 16 (bottom) © Bruce Mathews/
Midwestock; page 17 © 1997 David McGlynn/FPG International; page
17 (inset) © 1995 Mugshots/The Stock Market; page 18 © 1996
Chuck Savage/The Stock Market; page 19 © Tony Freeman/PhotoEdit;
page 20 David Muench/Stone; pages 22-23 Digital Stock; page 22
Courtesy of Cynthia Richardson; page 23 Courtesy of Korenne
Richardson; page 24 Donovan Reese/Stone; Back cover (top to bottom):
Used with permission of the Board of Trustees of the New Bedford Free
Public Library; © T. H. Benton and R. P. Benton Testamentary Trusts/
Licensed by VAGA, New York, NY; Brown Brothers, Sterling, PA; Culver
Pictures, NY; © Brenda Tharp/Photo Researchers, Inc., NY

MAP
National Geographic Society

Produced through the worldwide resources of the National Geographic
Society, John M. Fahey, Jr., President and Chief Executive Officer;
Gilbert M. Grosvenor, Chairman of the Board; Nina D. Hoffman,
Executive Vice President and President, Books and School Publishing.

PREPARED BY NATIONAL GEOGRAPHIC SCHOOL PUBLISHING
Ericka Markman, Vice President; Steve Mico, Editorial Director;
Marianne Hiland, Editorial Manager; Anita Schwartz, Project Editor;
Tara Peterson, Editorial Assistant; Jim Hiscott, Design Manager; Linda
McKnight, Art Director; Diana Bourdrez, Anne Whittle, Photo Research;
Matt Wascavage, Manager of Publishing Services; Sean Philpotts,
Production Coordinator; Jane Ponton, Production Artist.

Production: Clifton M. Brown III, Manufacturing and Quality Control.

PROGRAM DEVELOPMENT
Gare Thompson Associates, Inc.

Copyright © 2002 National Geographic Society. All Rights Reserved.

National Geographic Society, National Geographic School Publishing,
National Geographic Reading Expeditions, and the Yellow Border are
trademarks of the National Geographic Society.

Published by the National Geographic Society
1145 17th Street, N.W.
Washington, D.C. 20036-4688
ISBN: 978-0-7922-8697-4
ISBN: 0-7922-8697-9

6 7 8 9 10 11 12 19 18 17 16 15 14 13
Printed in the United States of America.

Table of Contents

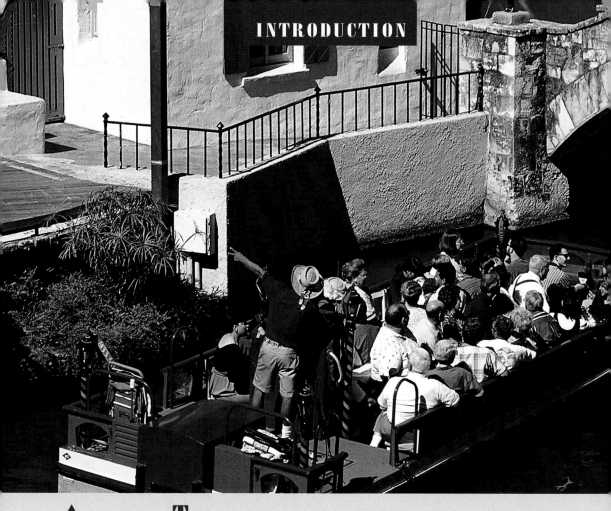

▲

Sight-seeing along the River Walk in San Antonio

The Gonzalez family lives in different communities all across the United States. They **communicate** through letter postcards, telephone calls, and e-mail. In this way, everyon knows what is happening with all the family members.

The head of the family is Paz Gonzalez. She lives in San Antonio, Texas. San Antonio is an old city. It was settled over 300 years ago. First, Native Americans settled along the San Antonio River. Later, the Spanish settled there and built a military post and a **mission,** a kind of church. In th early 1800s, American settlers moved to the area. Today, San Antonio is the eleventh largest city in the United State: Over 1,100,000 people call San Antonio home.

Cambria,
California

Lawrence,
Kansas

San Antonio,
Texas

...z's granddaughter, Lina Gonzalez, lives near the
...wn of Cambria, California. Her parents, Joe and
...ula, own an avocado farm. The farm is close to the
...cific Ocean. Avocados grow well in the mild climate.

...z's grandson, Gil Salas, lives in the Midwest. His
...rents, Raul and Angela, teach at universities in
...wrence, Kansas. Lawrence is a smaller city than San
...ntonio. About 80,000 people, including university
...dents, live in Lawrence.

CHAPTER 1

Paz's Community
San Antonio, Texas

I am taking photographs of San Antonio for my grandchildren. I'm going to make an album of their favorite places. Lina and Gil love to come here to Paseo del Rio, the River Walk. We eat lunch at one of the many restaurants along the River Walk. We watch the **tourists** and try to guess where they are from. Usually Lina guesses right. She says she can tell where people are from by how they dress and talk. San Antonio is a big tourist town!

Next I take a picture of the Tower of the Americas. This huge tower is 750 feet tall. It's one of Lina and Gil's favorite places in San Antonio. When Gil and Lina first took the glass elevator to the top, they closed their eyes for the whole ride. Now they love it. They each try to spot the most things.

From the observation deck, you can see almost all of San Antonio. You can't miss the Alamodome. That's where we watch soccer, football, and basketball games—and even ice skating.

▶

Tower of the Americas

ext I'm going to Market Square. El Mercado, the largest
exican market in the United States, is in Market Square.
n Antonio is about 150 miles north of Mexico. Like me,
bout half the population in the city is Mexican American.
he last time Gil, Lina, and I were here, we bought a
ñata and pan dulce, or sweet bread.

ddenly I hear a loud roar. I look up and see four jets
flying high above me. A man next to me salutes the
planes. He tells me he is visiting his son, a pilot at
Randolph Air Force Base. I smile. He is very proud of
his son. Many people here in San Antonio work for the
military. They say if you don't work for the military,
you work for the tourist industry.

Food and crafts at a Mexican fair
▼

Now I'm off to the Alamo. The Alamo is an old mission that was changed into a **fort**. Gil likes to visit the Alamo. He thinks you can still hear the famous battle that raged around it during the Texas Revolution. Gil did a report on the Alamo for school last year. He wrote about Davy Crockett, Jim Bowie, and all the other Texan rebels who lost their lives when Mexican soldiers attacked the fort. He got an A on his report, too!

As I walk back to my car, I realize how much I miss my family. I have many stories to tell them. Then an idea hits me. We'll have a family **reunion**! I can't wait to get home.

I live in a neighborhood called Southtown. I love it here. Southtown is a mix of houses, restaurants, and old warehouses. The warehouses have so much space that artists now live and work in many of them.

I race into my house to e-mail my children and grandchildren across the United States. I tell them to come to San Antonio for a family reunion!

◀ **After a 13-day battle, the Alamo fell to Mexican forces.**

CHAPTER 2

Lina's Community
Cambria, California

help my mom and dad load the truck with boxes of avocados. The name of our farm—Gold Creek Farm—is spelled out on the sides of the boxes. Through the holes in the boxes, I can see the avocados' dark green, rough skins. I think avocados are funny looking, but I love how they taste!

Wooded foothills rise behind our farm. When I take a deep breath, I can smell the ocean. The Pacific Ocean is about 12 miles away. The ocean helps cool the air, but our farm hardly ever gets any fog. On the other side of the foothills and the mountains is the desert. Gold Creek Farm is in a good place for growing avocados.

It's Thursday. Like the other farmers in the area, we take our produce to the farmers' market every Thursday. The market is hard work, but it's also fun.

A sea otter swims mostly on its back.

I hop into the truck between my parents. We drive down the road between Monterey pines. The tall pines protect the avocado trees from the wind. I'm excited abou my grandmother Paz's e-mail about a family reunion. "Can we go to San Antonio?" I ask my parents.

"If we can find the time," Dad tells me. "We'll be **harvesting** the avocados through April. Then we have to make all our deliveries." I help my parents deliver avocados to restaurants and grocery stores.

In ten minutes, we're in Cambria. This is where I go to school. The bus picks me up and takes me into town. Our school is not huge, but it is not tiny either.

Dad turns left, south onto Highway 1. The highway follows the California coast. Waves roll against the shore. look for whales, dolphins, and sea otters. Lots of times I spot sea otters. You can hear their loud cries from the road. Sometimes I see dolphins. From December to February, I see gray whales.

We reach the farmers' market in plenty of time
to set up our stand. We unpack our boxes of
avocados. Dad cuts open an avocado for me and
takes out the seed. He sprinkles each half with
lemon and a little bit of salt. I use a spoon to
scoop out the avocado.

The farmers' market is in downtown San Luis Obispo. The
market runs for several blocks along Higuera Street. By
6:00 p.m. the street is filled with all kinds of sights, smells,
sounds, and tastes! Even in winter, farmers sell vegetables,
flowers, and herbs.

A juggler tosses four avocados into the air. She keeps them
going, passing them from hand to hand, without dropping
one! Musicians play steel drums, guitars, and horns. Mom
and I dance to the music. Dad drums on the boxes.

"It would really be great to see Paz and cousin Gil," I say.
Mom pats my head. "We'll see." I cross my fingers and
smile at her. I hope we go!

11

By 9:30 p.m., the night air is cool. The farmers' market is closed. The back of our truck is now filled with empty boxes. As we drive north, I turn around. I see the lights of San Luis Obispo spread out. Cambria is a town, but San Luis Obispo is a city.

"San Antonio has a lot more people than San Luis Obispo, doesn't it?" I ask. San Antonio seems big and exciting to me.

"Maybe 43,000 people live in San Luis Obispo," Dad answers. "San Antonio has more than a million people."

"A million and one," I say. "Don't forget Paz."

Dad laughs. "You really do want to go to San Antonio, don't you? We'll see what we can do."

Highway 1 runs along the Pacific coastline.
▼

I'm sleepy so I rest my head against Mom's shoulder. An hour later, Mom wakes me up. We're driving down the dirt road to the farm. I can smell the ocean. The dark leaves of the avocado trees gleam in the moonlight.

CHAPTER 3

Gil's Community
Lawrence, Kansas

Looking out of my mother's office window, I can still see patches of snow. Lawrence usually gets at least 21 inches of snow in the winter. When the wind blows, it feels really cold. I wish it were warm like San Antonio.

I think about Lina on her avocado farm. There are some farms around Lawrence, but none of them grow avocados! Most farmers here grow wheat. Kansas is known as the "Wheat State" and the "Breadbasket of the Nation." Kansas farmers grow corn and soybeans, too.

▲ **Fraser Hall, University of Kansas**

My mom teaches math at the University of Kansas. People call it KU, for short. More people work at KU than at any other place in Lawrence. Lots of students live in Lawrence, too.

I see my dad waving. "Dad's here," I tell Mom. "I can't wait to tell him about the reunion." Mom tells me not to slam the door as I race out to meet him.

13

▲
This is a fossil of a fish that lived over 140 million years ago.

Today, we're going to visit the Natural History Museum at KU. Then we're going downtown to have lunch and shop. I tell Dad about the e-mail from Grandma Paz as we walk back to Mom's office. Dad smiles as I tell him about the reunion.

The museum is one of my favorite places. It always has lots of programs for kids. There are art programs, such as painting or drawing. There are science programs, too. I like the science ones the best. I like to do experiments.

Together, we wander through the snow to the museum. Inside, I stare at all the **fossils**. It's weird to see traces of animals and plants that lived long, long ago. I see fossils of fish, birds, and even reptiles!

Last spring, the museum led a fossil hunt field trip. I found the fossil of a fish near the Smoky Hill River in the middle of the state. It's hard to believe, but a long time ago, a sea covered parts of Kansas.

Leaving the museum, we walk to Massachusetts Street. It is always crowded downtown. "Mass" Street—everybody here calls it that—goes down to the river. The river is the Kansas River. Almost everybody in Kansas calls it the "Kaw" River.

Old and new buildings line the street. An old bank is now a restaurant. We have lunch there. Outside, someone is singing and playing a fiddle. Cowboys and settlers used to sing around the campfire. There are lots of songs about Kansas. My favorite is "Kansas Land."

After lunch, we stop at an art gallery. Many artists live in Lawrence. Dad says people here really like art and support artists, just like they do in Grandma Paz's neighborhood. One local artist, Stanley J. Herd, carved a 1,000-foot portrait of a Native American out of a field of wheat for Dad's school. Dad teaches at the Haskell Indian Nations University.

The artist Stan Herd created this giant portrait in a Kansas wheat field. ▼

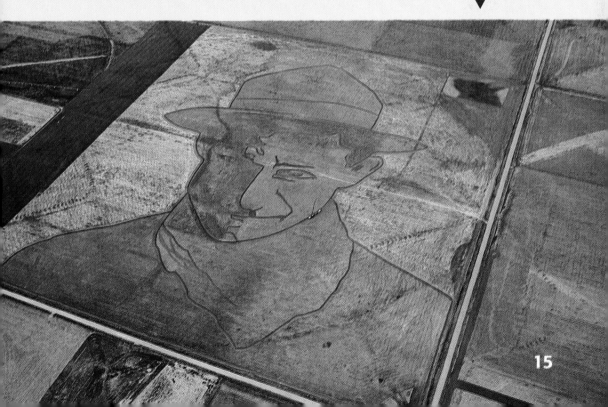

As we go home, I walk carefully in case there is ice on the sidewalk. The houses sit at the top of long steps. One of my best friends, Morgan, lives on the corner. Her parents work for the newspaper, the *Lawrence Journal-World*. Her dad goes to all the KU Jayhawk basketball games and then writes about them. He told us that Dr. James Naismith, who once taught physical education at KU, invented the game of basketball.

Morgan is waiting for me on her front porch. We meet Luke at my house. The three of us play basketball together all the time. We met last summer at a basketball camp. KU's head basketball coach and some of the Jayhawk team worked with us.

Allen Field House at KU
▼

I like living in Lawrence, even with all the snow. I love playing basketball. No matter how cold it gets outside, I'm always ready to shoot some hoops. I want to write about basketball when I grow up.

CHAPTER 4

The Gonzalez Family Reunion

Early in June, Lina and her family drive north along the coast to San Francisco. At the airport, they check their bags—and two cases of avocados. "Everybody in the Gonzalez family loves avocados," Lina tells the airline clerk.

Gil and his parents drive south from Lawrence to San Antonio. The trip takes them two days. Gil spots the Tower of the Americas on the San Antonio **skyline**. "We're almost there," he says.

At Paz's front door, Gil smells flour and corn tortillas cooking. Paz rushes to hug them all.

Soon it's time to pick up Lina and her family at the airport. Paz, Gil, Raul, and Angela take the busy highway that loops around San Antonio. Gil is the first one to see Lina, his Uncle Joe, and his Aunt Paula. "There they are!" he shouts. The Gonzalez family is together at last.

As you enter HemisFair Park, you see the Tower of the Americas.

17

Paz's Story

All my family is together in San Antonio! Everyone is at my house. My backyard is filled with cousins, uncles, aunts, brothers, sisters, and neighbors, too.

Lina's parents make a big bowl of guacamole. Gil's dad stirs a pot of frijoles, or beans, on the stove. His mom dips corn tortillas into a red chili sauce for enchiladas. Then Lina and Gil sprinkle onions and cheese on the tortillas and roll them up. An art student who lives across the street fills a piñata with toys and candy.

In the warm summer evening, we talk and laugh and eat. We sing and dance and tell stories. My grandchildren love my family stories.

Lina and Gil sprawl on the cool grass. They are full and happy. All around them, fireflies shine and crickets sing. It is warm. "Would you tell us about when you were little, Grandma?" Lina asks.

I smile and begin. "I was born in Terlingua, in 1935. Terlingua is in West Texas, near Big Bend National Park, not far from Mexico. It's in the desert. Mountains are all around. Terlingua was big and successful because of the mercury mines."

Joe explains, "They used to use mercury in thermometers and to help make things explode. It's very dangerous, but nobody knew that then."

"We lived in a small **adobe** house. My parents made the adobe bricks out of mud, hay, and water. Then they baked the bricks in the sun. Some people dug homes into the hills. West Texas is very dry. We would take pails to a big tank near the store and get our water there."

"What did you do for fun, Grandma?" Lina asks.

The Rio Grande flows through Big Bend National Park.
▼

"Oh, we'd ride our burros down to the river, to the Rio Grande. We'd go swimming. We'd count jackrabbits and antelope and deer. We'd look out for mountain lions. And after it rained, we'd pick wildflowers. We'd play games, like you do."

Gil smiles and says, "but not on the computer."

I shake my head. "There was one phone in Terlingua, and sometime it didn't work. In the 1940s, the mines closed. There wasn't much mercury left. People lost their jobs. They moved away. Terlingua became a ghost town. That's when my family and I moved here to San Antonio. My father got a job working for the railroad."

"Terlingua's not a ghost town anymore, is it?" asks Gil.

"No," I answer. "A lot of tourists visit Big Bend National Park and Terlingua now. They have a chili cook-off every year. People from all over the world come for the cook-off. Some people even fly their own planes to Terlingua."

"Do you miss living in Terlingua?" Lina asks me.

"I miss the mountains sometimes," I say. "But San Antonio is my home now. I like living in a city, but I wish I could see my family more often. I am happiest when we are all together."

The family is quiet for awhile. Raul passes around slices of watermelon. "You know," says Lina, "we should have a reunion every year. Next year, let's meet at Gold Creek Farm."

CHAPTER 5

Next Year, California!

Dear Grandma,

We had a great time at the family reunion! Mom, Dad, and I are busy planning next year's reunion at Gold Creek Farm. Here are some of the things we think the rest of the Gonzalez family might like to do:

1. Take a tour of the farm. We'll tell you all about growing and harvesting avocados.

2. Visit Moonstone Beach, which is just outside of Cambria. We can build sand castles and go swimming—if the water's not too cold!

3. Go to a real castle! A man named William Randolph Hearst built a huge house near here. Hearst Castle overlooks the Pacific Ocean. It's filled with art.

What do you think? I miss you!

Love, Lina

PM
26 JUL 93

USA 15

Buffalo Bill Cody

Mrs. Paz Gonzalez

210 Como Street

San Antonio, Texas 78265

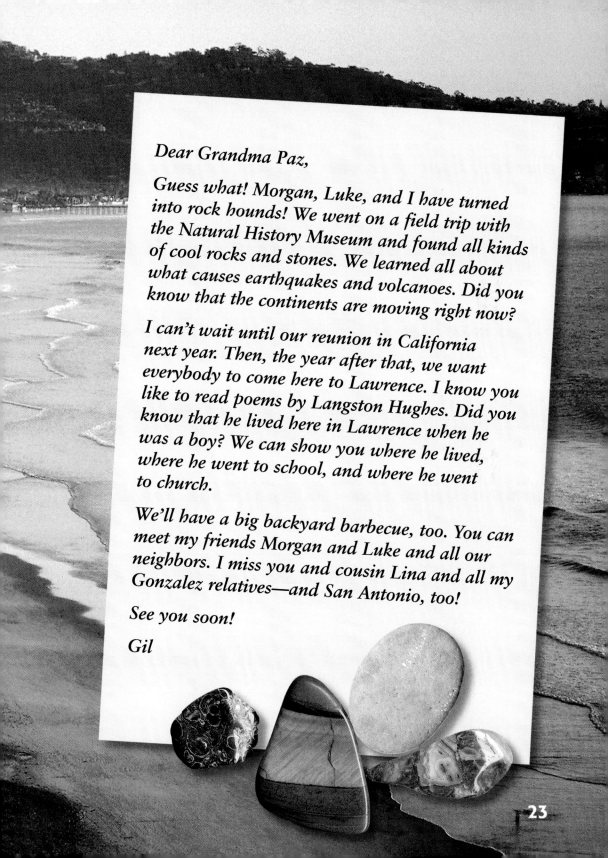

Dear Grandma Paz,

Guess what! Morgan, Luke, and I have turned into rock hounds! We went on a field trip with the Natural History Museum and found all kinds of cool rocks and stones. We learned all about what causes earthquakes and volcanoes. Did you know that the continents are moving right now?

I can't wait until our reunion in California next year. Then, the year after that, we want everybody to come here to Lawrence. I know you like to read poems by Langston Hughes. Did you know that he lived here in Lawrence when he was a boy? We can show you where he lived, where he went to school, and where he went to church.

We'll have a big backyard barbecue, too. You can meet my friends Morgan and Luke and all our neighbors. I miss you and cousin Lina and all my Gonzalez relatives—and San Antonio, too!

See you soon!

Gil

Glossary

adobe – a brick made of clay mixed with straw and dried in the sun

communicate – to share information, ideas, or feelings with another person by talking or writing

fort – a building that is strongly built and can be defended against attack by an enemy

fossil – the remains of an animal or plant that lived long ago, preserved as rock

harvest – to gather in a crop for use or for sale

mission – a church or other place where a religious group teaches that group's faith and does good works

reunion – a bringing together of family, friends, or other groups of people

skyline – the outline of buildings as seen against the sky

tourist – a person traveling to a place for pleasure